The Wine Book

HUGH LAUTER LEVIN ASSOCIATES, INC., NEW YORK

DISTRIBUTED BY
MACMILLAN PUBLISHING COMPANY

This book belongs to

_____

ILLUSTRATIONS

Antonio Casanova Y Estorach
MONK TESTING WINE
1886
oil on canvas
16⅛ × 12⅞″
The Brooklyn Museum; Bequest of Caroline H. Polhemus

Achille Pinelli
WINEMAKERS CARRYING GRAPES TO THE WINE PRESS
19th century
watercolor
Museum of Rome
Photograph: Giraudon/Art Resource

Juan Gris
BOTTLE, NEWSPAPER, AND FRUIT BOWL
1916
oil on panel
28½ × 19¾″
Öeffentliche Kunstsammlung Basel, Kunstmuseum

ATHENA SERVING WINE TO HERACLES
Attic dish,
c. 470 B.C.
Staatliche Antikensammlung und Glyptothek, Munich
Photograph: Caecilia H. Moessner, Munich

PRESSING OF GRAPES from *LES VENDAGES*
Loire region,
16th-century tapestry
Musée Cluny, Paris
Photograph: Giraudon/Art Resource

Calligraphy: Gunta Alexander

Picture Research: Ann Levy

© 1986 by Hugh Lauter Levin Associates, Inc.
All rights reserved.

Printed in Japan

ISBN 0-88363-087-7

Jan Vermeer
THE GLASS OF WINE
c. 1658–60
oil on canvas
25⅝ × 30¼″
Staatliche Museen Preussischer Kulturbesitz, Gemäldegalerie, Berlin

JOSHUA AND CALEB CARRYING A POLE WITH A BUNCH OF GRAPES depicted on a roemer
Dutch (engraved by "Hi")
1643
transparent light-green glass; blown, molded, diamond-engraved
The Corning Museum of Glass, Corning, New York; Gift of the Ruth Bryan Strauss Memorial Foundation

William Kalf
STILL LIFE
1663
oil on canvas
23¾ × 19¾″
The Cleveland Museum of Art; Purchase, Leonard C. Hanna Jr. Bequest

Preston Dickenson
STILL LIFE
undated
oil on canvas
24 × 30⅛″
The Cleveland Museum of Art; Hinman B. Hurlbut Collection

THE MONTH OF OCTOBER from *THE CYCLE OF THE MONTHS*
c. 1400
fresco
Torre dell'Aquila of the Castello del Buonconsiglio, Trento, Italy
Photograph: SCALA/Art Resource

THE FOUR SEASONS
THE ENCYCLOPEDIA OF MAURUIS RABANUS
1028
Abbazia, Montecassino, Italy
Photograph: SCALA/Art Resource

Pierre Auguste Renoir
THE LUNCHEON OF THE BOATING PARTY
1881
oil on canvas
51 × 68″
The Phillips Collection, Washington

Constant Troyon
GRAPE HARVEST AT SURESNES
Musée Municipal, Limoges
Photograph: Giraudon/Art Resource

Contents

MONK TESTING WINE—*Antonio Casanova Y Estorach*

Each wine holds its own special secrets, generously revealed to us as we drink and sometimes remembered long afterward.

When we recall a wine we have tasted, we conjure up not only the impressions recorded by our senses – color, bouquet, taste – but also our memories of the occasion. When we think of a special wine, we relive a feast with friends, the delight of sharing a favorite bottle with a loved one, the scenery and atmosphere surrounding the discovery of a new wine.

This book is designed to be a personal record in which you can capture and preserve the magic of wine. Your cellar notes, tasting notes, and records of extraordinary meals will refresh your memories of favorite wines.

The Wine Cellar

History

Location _____

_____

Date Started _____

Capacity _____

First Wines _____

_____

_____

_____

_____

_____

Comments _____

_____

_____

_____

_____

_____

_____

The Wine Cellar

The Cellar Plan

Diagram your cellar below,
with wine locations marked.

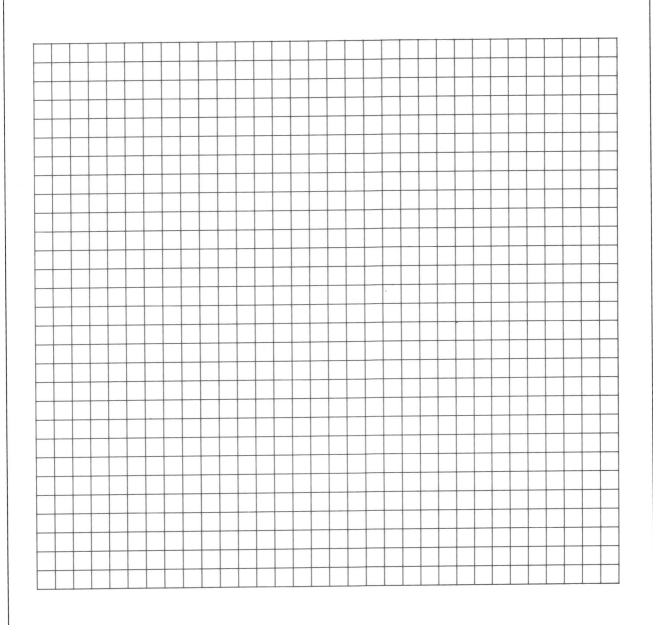

The Wine Cellar

Cellar Notes

Wine			Vintage
Source			Cellar Location
Date Purchased		Quantity	Price

Date Used	Quantity Used	Balance	Occasion/Guests/Food Served/ Comments/Page No. for Tasting Notes

Wine			Vintage
Source			Cellar Location
Date Purchased		Quantity	Price

Date Used	Quantity Used	Balance	Occasion/Guests/Food Served/ Comments/Page No. for Tasting Notes

Wine			Vintage
Source			Cellar Location
Date Purchased		Quantity	Price

Date Used	Quantity Used	Balance	Occasion/Guests/Food Served/ Comments/Page No. for Tasting Notes

WINEMAKERS CARRYING GRAPES TO THE WINE PRESS—Achille Pinelli

The Wine Cellar

Cellar Notes

Wine				Vintage
Source				Cellar Location
Date Purchased		Quantity		Price

Date Used	Quantity Used	Balance	Occasion/Guests/Food Served/ Comments/Page No. for Tasting Notes

Wine				Vintage
Source				Cellar Location
Date Purchased		Quantity		Price

Date Used	Quantity Used	Balance	Occasion/Guests/Food Served/ Comments/Page No. for Tasting Notes

Wine				Vintage
Source				Cellar Location
Date Purchased		Quantity		Price

Date Used	Quantity Used	Balance	Occasion/Guests/Food Served/ Comments/Page No. for Tasting Notes

The Wine Cellar

Cellar Notes

Wine			Vintage
Source			Cellar Location
Date Purchased		Quantity	Price

Date Used	Quantity Used	Balance	Occasion/Guests/Food Served/ Comments/Page No. for Tasting Notes

Wine			Vintage
Source			Cellar Location
Date Purchased		Quantity	Price

Date Used	Quantity Used	Balance	Occasion/Guests/Food Served/ Comments/Page No. for Tasting Notes

Wine			Vintage
Source			Cellar Location
Date Purchased		Quantity	Price

Date Used	Quantity Used	Balance	Occasion/Guests/Food Served/ Comments/Page No. for Tasting Notes

The Wine Cellar

Cellar Notes

Wine			Vintage
Source			Cellar Location
Date Purchased		Quantity	Price

Date Used	Quantity Used	Balance	Occasion/Guests/Food Served/ Comments/Page No. for Tasting Notes

Wine			Vintage
Source			Cellar Location
Date Purchased		Quantity	Price

Date Used	Quantity Used	Balance	Occasion/Guests/Food Served/ Comments/Page No. for Tasting Notes

Wine			Vintage
Source			Cellar Location
Date Purchased		Quantity	Price

Date Used	Quantity Used	Balance	Occasion/Guests/Food Served/ Comments/Page No. for Tasting Notes

BOTTLE, NEWSPAPER, AND FRUIT BOWL—*Juan Gris*

The Wine Cellar

Cellar Notes

Wine				Vintage
Source				Cellar Location
Date Purchased		Quantity		Price

Date Used	Quantity Used	Balance	Occasion/Guests/Food Served/ Comments/Page No. for Tasting Notes

Wine				Vintage
Source				Cellar Location
Date Purchased		Quantity		Price

Date Used	Quantity Used	Balance	Occasion/Guests/Food Served/ Comments/Page No. for Tasting Notes

Wine				Vintage
Source				Cellar Location
Date Purchased		Quantity		Price

Date Used	Quantity Used	Balance	Occasion/Guests/Food Served/ Comments/Page No. for Tasting Notes

The Wine Cellar

Cellar Notes

Wine			Vintage
Source			Cellar Location
Date Purchased		Quantity	Price

Date Used	Quantity Used	Balance	Occasion/Guests/Food Served/ Comments/Page No. for Tasting Notes

Wine			Vintage
Source			Cellar Location
Date Purchased		Quantity	Price

Date Used	Quantity Used	Balance	Occasion/Guests/Food Served/ Comments/Page No. for Tasting Notes

Wine			Vintage
Source			Cellar Location
Date Purchased		Quantity	Price

Date Used	Quantity Used	Balance	Occasion/Guests/Food Served/ Comments/Page No. for Tasting Notes

The Wine Cellar

Cellar Notes

Wine				Vintage
Source				Cellar Location
Date Purchased		Quantity		Price

Date Used	Quantity Used	Balance	Occasion/Guests/Food Served/ Comments/Page No. for Tasting Notes

Wine				Vintage
Source				Cellar Location
Date Purchased		Quantity		Price

Date Used	Quantity Used	Balance	Occasion/Guests/Food Served/ Comments/Page No. for Tasting Notes

Wine				Vintage
Source				Cellar Location
Date Purchased		Quantity		Price

Date Used	Quantity Used	Balance	Occasion/Guests/Food Served/ Comments/Page No. for Tasting Notes

The Wine Cellar

Cellar Notes

Wine			Vintage			
Source			Cellar Location			
Date Purchased		Quantity	Price			

Date Used	Quantity Used	Balance	Occasion/Guests/Food Served/ Comments/Page No. for Tasting Notes

Wine			Vintage			
Source			Cellar Location			
Date Purchased		Quantity	Price			

Date Used	Quantity Used	Balance	Occasion/Guests/Food Served/ Comments/Page No. for Tasting Notes

Wine			Vintage			
Source			Cellar Location			
Date Purchased		Quantity	Price			

Date Used	Quantity Used	Balance	Occasion/Guests/Food Served/ Comments/Page No. for Tasting Notes

The Wine Cellar

Cellar Notes

Wine			Vintage
Source			Cellar Location
Date Purchased		Quantity	Price

Date Used	Quantity Used	Balance	Occasion/Guests/Food Served/ Comments/Page No. for Tasting Notes

Wine			Vintage
Source			Cellar Location
Date Purchased		Quantity	Price

Date Used	Quantity Used	Balance	Occasion/Guests/Food Served/ Comments/Page No. for Tasting Notes

Wine			Vintage
Source			Cellar Location
Date Purchased		Quantity	Price

Date Used	Quantity Used	Balance	Occasion/Guests/Food Served/ Comments/Page No. for Tasting Notes

ATHENA SERVING WINE TO HERACLES—Attic dish

The Wine Cellar

Cellar Notes

Wine			Vintage	
Source			Cellar Location	
Date Purchased		Quantity	Price	

Date Used	Quantity Used	Balance	Occasion/Guests/Food Served/ Comments/Page No. for Tasting Notes

Wine			Vintage	
Source			Cellar Location	
Date Purchased		Quantity	Price	

Date Used	Quantity Used	Balance	Occasion/Guests/Food Served/ Comments/Page No. for Tasting Notes

Wine			Vintage	
Source			Cellar Location	
Date Purchased		Quantity	Price	

Date Used	Quantity Used	Balance	Occasion/Guests/Food Served/ Comments/Page No. for Tasting Notes

The Wine Cellar

Cellar Notes

Wine			Vintage
Source			Cellar Location
Date Purchased		Quantity	Price

Date Used	Quantity Used	Balance	Occasion/Guests/Food Served/ Comments/Page No. for Tasting Notes

Wine			Vintage
Source			Cellar Location
Date Purchased		Quantity	Price

Date Used	Quantity Used	Balance	Occasion/Guests/Food Served/ Comments/Page No. for Tasting Notes

Wine			Vintage
Source			Cellar Location
Date Purchased		Quantity	Price

Date Used	Quantity Used	Balance	Occasion/Guests/Food Served/ Comments/Page No. for Tasting Notes

The Wine Cellar

Cellar Notes

Wine			Vintage
Source			Cellar Location
Date Purchased		Quantity	Price

Date Used	Quantity Used	Balance	Occasion/Guests/Food Served/ Comments/Page No. for Tasting Notes

Wine			Vintage
Source			Cellar Location
Date Purchased		Quantity	Price

Date Used	Quantity Used	Balance	Occasion/Guests/Food Served/ Comments/Page No. for Tasting Notes

Wine			Vintage
Source			Cellar Location
Date Purchased		Quantity	Price

Date Used	Quantity Used	Balance	Occasion/Guests/Food Served/ Comments/Page No. for Tasting Notes

PRESSING OF GRAPES—16th-century French

The Wine Cellar

Cellar Notes

Wine			Vintage
Source			Cellar Location
Date Purchased		Quantity	Price

Date Used	Quantity Used	Balance	Occasion/Guests/Food Served/ Comments/Page No. for Tasting Notes

Wine			Vintage
Source			Cellar Location
Date Purchased		Quantity	Price

Date Used	Quantity Used	Balance	Occasion/Guests/Food Served/ Comments/Page No. for Tasting Notes

Wine			Vintage
Source			Cellar Location
Date Purchased		Quantity	Price

Date Used	Quantity Used	Balance	Occasion/Guests/Food Served/ Comments/Page No. for Tasting Notes

The Wine Cellar

Cellar Notes

Wine			Vintage	
Source			Cellar Location	
Date Purchased		Quantity	Price	

Date Used	Quantity Used	Balance	Occasion/Guests/Food Served/ Comments/Page No. for Tasting Notes

Wine			Vintage	
Source			Cellar Location	
Date Purchased		Quantity	Price	

Date Used	Quantity Used	Balance	Occasion/Guests/Food Served/ Comments/Page No. for Tasting Notes

Wine			Vintage	
Source			Cellar Location	
Date Purchased		Quantity	Price	

Date Used	Quantity Used	Balance	Occasion/Guests/Food Served/ Comments/Page No. for Tasting Notes

Tasting Notes

Good wine maketh good blood,
Good blood causeth good humors,
Good humors cause good thoughts,
Good thoughts bring forth good works,
Good works carry a man to heaven;
Ergo, good wine carrieth a man to heaven. —*Anonymous*

Wine _____ Vintage _____

Source _____ Price _____

Place Tasted _____ Date _____

Occasion _____

With whom _____

_____

Appearance _____

Bouquet _____

Taste _____

Body & Balance _____

Comments _____

_____

_____

_____

THE GLASS OF WINE—Jan Vermeer

*Wine rejoices the heart of men,
and joy is the mother of virtue.*
— Goethe

Wine _____ Vintage _____

Source _____ Price _____

Place Tasted _____ Date _____

Occasion _____

With whom _____

_____

Appearance _____

Bouquet _____

Taste _____

Body & Balance _____

Comments _____

_____

_____

_____

Tasting Notes

With bread and wine you can walk your road.
— Spanish Proverb

Wine ——————— Vintage ———
Source ——————— Price ———
Place Tasted ——————— Date ———
Occasion ———————————
With whom ———————————

Appearance ———————————
Bouquet ———————————
Taste ———————————
Body & Balance ———————————
Comments ———————————

———————————

———————————

———————————

A meal without wine is like a day without sunshine.
—Anthelme Brillant-Savarin

Wine _____ Vintage _____

Source _____ Price _____

Place Tasted _____ Date _____

Occasion _____

With whom _____

_____

Appearance _____

Bouquet _____

Taste _____

Body & Balance _____

Comments _____

_____

_____

_____

JOSHUA AND CALEB CARRYING A POLE WITH A BUNCH OF GRAPES—Dutch engraving

Wine that maketh glad the heart of man.
—Psalms

Wine _____ Vintage _____

Source _____ Price _____

Place Tasted _____ Date _____

Occasion _____

With whom _____

_____

Appearance _____

Bouquet _____

Taste _____

Body & Balance _____

Comments _____

_____

_____

_____

Never did a noble man dislike good wine.
—Rabelais

Wine _____ Vintage _____

Source _____ Price _____

Place Tasted _____ Date _____

Occasion _____

With whom _____

_____

Appearance _____

Bouquet _____

Taste _____

Body & Balance _____

Comments _____

_____

_____

_____

Tasting Notes

Burgundy for kings,
Champagne for duchesses,
and
Claret for gentlemen. —French Proverb

Wine ———————— Vintage ————
Source ————————— Price ————
Place Tasted ————— Date ————
Occasion ————————————
With whom ———————————

————————————————

Appearance ————————————
Bouquet ——————————————
Taste ————————————————
Body & Balance ————————————
Comments ——————————————

————————————————

————————————————

————————————————

STILL LIFE—William Kalf

Tasting Notes

Fill ev'ry glass, for wine inspires us,
And fires us
With courage, love, and joy.
—John Gay

Wine _____ Vintage _____

Source _____ Price _____

Place Tasted _____ Date _____

Occasion _____

With whom _____

_____

Appearance _____

Bouquet _____

Taste _____

Body & Balance _____

Comments _____

_____

_____

_____

On turnpikes of wonder wine leads the mind forth.
—Hafiz

Wine ———————— Vintage ————
Source ———————— Price ————
Place Tasted ———————— Date ————
Occasion ————————————
With whom ————————————

Appearance ————————————
Bouquet ————————————
Taste ————————————
Body & Balance ————————————
Comments ————————————

————————————

————————————

————————————

Tasting Notes

The sensibility of wine resembles that of Man.
It must go through a critical phase, which it must
then forget in order to recall its happy years.

—Voltaire

Wine _____ Vintage _____

Source _____ Price _____

Place Tasted _____ Date _____

Occasion _____

With whom _____

_____

Appearance _____

Bouquet _____

Taste _____

Body & Balance _____

Comments _____

_____

_____

_____

STILL LIFE—Preston Dickenson

Tasting Notes

*Of all the vegetable kingdom, the vine alone
makes intelligible the true savor of the earth.*
—Colette

Wine _____ Vintage _____
Source _____ Price _____
Place Tasted _____ Date _____
Occasion _____
With whom _____

_____

Appearance _____
Bouquet _____
Taste _____
Body & Balance _____
Comments _____

_____

_____

_____

Tasting Notes

Wine is a peep-hole on a man.
—Alcaeus

Wine _____ Vintage _____
Source _____ Price _____
Place Tasted _____ Date _____
Occasion _____
With whom _____

_____

Appearance _____
Bouquet _____
Taste _____
Body & Balance _____
Comments _____

_____

_____

_____

Tasting Notes

May our love be like good wine;
Grow stronger
As it grows older.   —English Toast

Wine _____ Vintage _____
Source _____ Price _____
Place Tasted _____ Date _____
Occasion _____
With whom _____

_____

Appearance _____
Bouquet _____
Taste _____
Body & Balance _____
Comments _____

_____

_____

_____

THE MONTH OF OCTOBER—*Italian fresco*

Tasting Notes

*Quickly, bring me a beaker of wine, so that I may
wet my mind and say something clever.*
—Aristophanes

Wine _____ Vintage _____
Source _____ Price _____
Place Tasted _____ Date _____
Occasion _____
With whom _____
_____
Appearance _____
Bouquet _____
Taste _____
Body & Balance _____
Comments _____
_____
_____
_____

Tasting Notes

A Book of Verses underneath the Bough,
A Jug of Wine, a Loaf of Bread—and Thou
Beside me singing in the Wilderness—
Oh, Wilderness were Paradise enow!

—Edward Fitzgerald
"The Rubaiyat of Omar Khayyam"

Wine _____ Vintage _____

Source _____ Price _____

Place Tasted _____ Date _____

Occasion _____

With whom _____

_____

Appearance _____

Bouquet _____

Taste _____

Body & Balance _____

Comments _____

_____

_____

_____

Tasting Notes

Good wine is a good familiar
creature if it be well used.
—Shakespeare

Wine _____ Vintage _____
Source _____ Price _____
Place Tasted _____ Date _____
Occasion _____
With whom _____

_____

Appearance _____
Bouquet _____
Taste _____
Body & Balance _____
Comments _____

_____

_____

_____

THE FOUR SEASONS—German codex

Tasting Notes

From wine what sudden friendship springs!
—John Gay

Wine _____ Vintage _____

Source _____ Price _____

Place Tasted _____ Date _____

Occasion _____

With whom _____

_____

Appearance _____

Bouquet _____

Taste _____

Body & Balance _____

Comments _____

_____

_____

_____

Tasting Notes

If all be true that I do think,
There are five reasons we should drink:
Good wine – a friend – or being dry –
Or lest we should be by and by –
Or any other reason why.

—Henry Aldrich

Wine _____ Vintage _____

Source _____ Price _____

Place Tasted _____ Date _____

Occasion _____

With whom _____

_____

Appearance _____

Bouquet _____

Taste _____

Body & Balance _____

Comments _____

_____

_____

_____

Labels of Favorite Wines

# Labels of Favorite Wines

 # *Labels of Favorite Wines*

A Memorable Meal

Occasion _____

Place _____ Date _____

Guests _____

_____

_____

_____

_____

First Courses _____

Wine _____

_____

Main Course _____

Wine _____

_____

Salad/Cheeses _____

Wine _____

_____

Dessert _____

Wine _____

THE LUNCHEON OF THE BOATING PARTY—*Pierre Auguste Renoir*

A Memorable Meal

Occasion _____

Place _____ Date _____

Guests _____

_____

_____

_____

_____

First Courses _____

Wine _____

Main Course _____

Wine _____

Salad/Cheeses _____

Wine _____

Dessert _____

Wine _____

A Memorable Meal

Occasion _____

Place _____ Date _____

Guests _____

_____

_____

_____

First Courses _____

Wine _____

Main Course _____

Wine _____

Salad/Cheeses _____

Wine _____

Dessert _____

Wine _____

Vineyard Visits

Vineyard _____ Date _____

Location _____

Our Host _____

Wines Tasted _____

_____

Comments _____

_____

_____

_____

Vineyard _____ Date _____

Location _____

Our Host _____

Wines Tasted _____

_____

Comments _____

_____

_____

_____

GRAPE HARVEST AT SURESNES—*Constant Troyon*

Vineyard Visits

Vineyard _____ Date _____

Location _____

Our Host _____

Wines Tasted _____

_____

Comments _____

_____

_____

_____

Vineyard _____ Date _____

Location _____

Our Host _____

Wines Tasted _____

_____

Comments _____

_____

_____

_____

Vineyard _____ Date _____

Location _____

Our Host _____

Wines Tasted _____

_____

Comments _____

_____

_____

_____

Vineyard _____ Date _____

Location _____

Our Host _____

Wines Tasted _____

_____

Comments _____

_____

_____

_____

Wine Terms

Appearance

Clarity
Brilliant
Clear
Cloudy
Dull

Color–White
Amber
Gold
Green-Tinged
Straw
Yellow

Color–Red
Garnet
Mahogany
Purple
Red-Brown
Ruby

Color–Rosé
Deep Rose
Light Rose
Onion Skin
Partridge Eye

Bouquet/Taste

Acetic
Alcoholic
Almondy
Astringent
Bitter
Caramel
Corky
Dusty
Earthy
Flowery
Fruity
Grassy
Lingering
Long
Metallic
Musty
Nutty
Oaky
Piquant
Pungent
Short
Sour
Spicy
Tannic
Tart
Toasty

Body/Balance

Body
Fat
Full-Bodied
Heavy
Lean
Light
Massive
Medium
Thin
Viscous

Balance
Awkward
Harmonious
Unbalanced
Well-Balanced

General Descriptive Words

Aromatic	Elegant	Overripe
Assertive	Exotic	Powerful
Austere	Expansive	Refreshing
Big	Fragrant	Rich
Bland	Fresh	Robust
Bright	Generous	Rough
Clean	Hard	Sharp
Closed-In	Hearty	Smooth
Crisp	Immature	Supple
Delicate	Lush	Unctuous
Dense	Mature	Velvety
Dull	Mellow	Vigorous

Wine Merchants, Cellar Suppliers, Glassware & Accessories Merchants, Wine Clubs & Organizations

Pino Noir - Carneros   Acacia, Saintsbury

Hanzell, Richioli, Au Bon Climat

Williams Selyem

Cab   - Stags Leap (voluptuous)

Rutherford, Shafer

Clos Du Val, Kenwood

Diamond Creek

Mayacamus (bold)

Chard - Grgich Hills, Matanzas Creek

Trefethen (also Riesling), Jorpé

Sonoma-Cutrer, Au Bon Climat

Zin   - Sausal, Kenwood, Nalle, Limira

Rafanelli, Ravenswood, Amador Foothill

Santino

Try: Mosby   Brunello di Santa Barbara   (Sangiovese wine)
M+. Eden anything; also Ridge, Renaissance

64